How to Wholesale Real Estate

How to Get Started Investing in Real Estate with No Money Down and Massive Profits with Wholesaling

By

Income Mastery

publisher or author of this book can be held responsible for any difficulties or damages that may occur to them after making the information presented here.

In addition, the information on the following pages is intended for informational purposes only and should therefore be regarded as universal. As befits its nature, it is presented without warranty with respect to its prolonged validity or provisional quality. The trademarks mentioned are made without written consent and can in no way be considered as sponsorship of the same.

Table of Contents

Chapter 1: Real Estate... What is it? What is it?

The basic tax accounting dictionary defines real estate as things that cannot be transported from one place to another, such as land and mines and those that adhere permanently to them, such as buildings, constructions, houses, and trees.

Understanding this meaning we can say that real estate is considered to be any construction that is intimately attached to the ground, either in legal or physical form, that is, they are legally inseparable. Vessels, boats or aquatic aircraft are also considered as real estate, since their full functionality is linked to the maritime surface, being useless if they are detached from this surface. Special mention is made of mines and railway tracks, since they are constructions whose main attraction is the construction itself, either because they are the origin of the attraction or because they are the product of reference for economic activity.

Although real estate is considered a safe and low-risk investment. Many people who have decided to invest in real estate have lost a lot of money, either because they bought a property in a very bad location, because they couldn't find someone to rent it to after buying the property, or because they have to make repairs or remodels that end up being more expensive than they originally imagined and only caused them losses.

This is why before starting in the world of real estate investments, certain points must be considered to avoid putting your investment in risk.

ADVICE

1. **Analyze deeply the unit you plan to buy and make a budget of the total investment it will mean.** Always take consider Risk/Benefit values such as the location of the property, the price, the status at the time of the purchase, the need for repairs or remodeling of the property, the maintenance that will be necessary, the taxes that should be paid in time, the credit necessary to be able to acquire the property and above all, the possibility that allows the property to be sold quickly or rented at a price that justifies the amount invested in it.

2. **Think of them as long-term investments.** Don't sell too early. Investments in real estate are mostly long-term investments, some maybe medium term but are never considered short term investments. That is why we must consider that the profits obtained through the investment in real estate, will be seen in the long term. Remember that the capital gain of a property is subject to time and the real estate market.

3. Calculate the profitability of the property before investing. To find the best investment option it

is necessary to consider the profitability and it is also advisable to take other factors such as risk.

The formula to find the profitability of a property is:

Profitability = (Profit / Investment) x 100

In order to calculate the profitability of a property, one must take into account the investment of the property and the profit it has generated, which will be the difference between the investment value (Purchase) and the liquidation value (Sale) or, in the case of renting it, the difference between income and expenses (cash flow).

For example, if a property had an investment of US$30,000, and then sells for US$40,000, the profitability of the property would have been (40000 - 30000 / 30000) x 100 = 33.3%.

If a property had an investment of US$30,000, the income from rent in one year was US$12,000, and expenses in the same period were US$10,000, the profitability of the property will have been of (12000 – 10000 / 30000) x 100 = 6.7%.

4. **Diversify investment.** This is very important, not to invest everything in the same market, for someone who invests in the world of real estate, diversification can occur in making different purchases of real estate much cheaper and rent

them, than putting everything in a single investment of much more expensive property.

5. **Pre-sale is the key.** Seek to invest in real estate projects with pre-sale prices, which allows you to have an even greater return for being a long-term sale.

6. **Make sure the papers of the property are in order.** When purchasing a property, a certificate of freedom from encumbrances must be required to be able to take effective possession of the property. To have the titles of property and use of the property, also you must demand the plans of it where the limits of the property are specified.

7. **If it is going to be rented, you must make sure that there are guarantees.** You must have information about the people who want to rent the property, look for many references about the tenant, look for honorable people.

8. **When investing in a property that is under construction, you must see that the company in charge of the construction has finances that guarantee that the work is finished**. You can also get a building permit and a wastewater discharge permit.

9. **You must be careful with areas without added value**. In a place where there is a lot of real estates, the price of this does not grow but decreases, there are several factors that can limit the increase in value, including the construction of roads and the lack of planning to cope with a load of vehicle traffic.

10. **Analyze the market before you see a property.** Before you buy or lend money, look for market information. It may happen that rents in the area have risen in recent years, but you should know how much potential there is in the area for investment. If rents are high, but there are very few commercial premises, offices or empty dwellings, this will be an indication that the area still has the potential for growth, indicating that it is a good place to invest.

A property is an asset that joins the ground inseparably, physically and legally, real estate can separate them into 3 (three) different groups: Residential, commercial and industrial.

- Residential: undeveloped land, houses, condominiums, etc.

- Commercial: Office buildings, warehouses, retail store buildings, etc.

- Industrial: Factories, mines, farms, etc.

There are two types of rights in real estate

Real Estate: Personal Property. Includes intangible assets such as bonds, stocks or other investments. This also includes tangible goods such as furniture, computers, beds, clothing.

Real State is within the Real property. Real property is a lesser term which includes real estate plus a series of rights over it, this set of rights includes the owner using his property as he pleases.

The set of rights that the owner of a property has is divided into 5.

1. Possession: the right to occupy a property.

2. Enjoy: the right to use the property without external interference.

3. Control: The right to determine one's interests.

4. Exclusion: the right to reject the other's interests.

5. Disposition: The right to determine whether a property is sold or transferred to another party and in what form.

Real estate assets can have mortgages while furniture cannot and can be written into the public records of the property for greater legal control.

Chapter 2: What are REITs?

There are a variety of ways to invest in real estate, one of them is investing in real estate trusts or well known as REITs.

For those who are not interested in taking charge of a property, there are REITs, which offer the opportunity to participate directly in the property or the financing of real estate projects. These can generate real estate rents on the investment of office buildings, apartments, shopping malls, hotels, and warehouses. Many of these REITs focus on a single real estate investment system.

Most investors opt for REITs because of their high rate of return, although they are generally fully taxable, all real estate sectors are affected by different economic cycles, which is why REITs are intensified in the investment of a single sector. Smaller REITs have greater volatility, but you can get more growth potential with them.

What does investing in REITs offer us?

The main advantage is that through REITs, anyone can access investment in the real estate sector, with a wide portfolio of properties, diversified, with all its advantages and without the inconvenience of buying real estate directly (large capital, lack of liquidity, etc.).

Also, through the purchase of shares of REITs, not only are you buying the real estate assets in your portfolio, but you are buying a complete business that also includes an experienced management team specialized in optimizing and maximizing your profit for us.

We are not the ones who have to value the assets, buy them and then manage them, it is a complete pack.

An example of this experience can be seen in how most REITs managed the brutal "subprime mortgage" crisis in 2007-2008 in the USA, an ingredient cocktail that led to a "perfect storm in the sector" and one of the worst in a living memory, which has even been compared to that of the year 29. A crisis that left many corpses in the real estate sector, but that most REITs overcame with a conservative strategy on the part of their managers: reasonable debt ratios, along with capital increases and dividend cuts in some cases to release cash-flow with which to further lower debt ratios and avoid problems in their viability.

A study conducted in January 2011 commented that dividends had been cut in the sector by around 35% from the 2006-2007 peak. Of course, we talk about the average, in many cases, there was no cut but continued to increase that dividend, so it is important to select the best companies within the sector.

On the other hand, several studies show that REITs are a great long-term investment, with somewhat lower volatility, higher yield and dividend yield than the average of listed companies, so they fit perfectly with our long-term portfolio that will provide us with income for our retirement.

The correlation between REITs and the equity market, in general, is relatively low, usually between 0.55 and 0.65, which means that they will not fully follow the evolution of the general market and can often serve as a counterweight that stabilizes our portfolio a little.

The somewhat lower volatility can be explained by two reasons. The first is the relative ease of forecasting your cash flows, knowing how your business is going to evolve in the short or medium-term facilitates its valuation by analysts, which avoids many surprises in presentations of results and large deviations, for better or worse.

On the other hand, having an attractive return through dividends makes investors more patient in falls and there is no panic and big "sell-off" in major stock market crises.

All this does not mean that they are a risk-free asset; in fact, the drop-in rates that we have seen in recent years has made this type of securities with a predictable flow of income, become an alternative to bonds, convertibles and medium- to long-term fixed income that were giving very low yields.

Now that interest rates seem to be rising again, this type of stock loses interest for these investors and exits them, which is causing large price falls. Times are changing and it doesn't mean that everything will stay the same for life, we will always have to be vigilant about our investments.

What must a REITs comply with and what advantages does it have?

For a company to be considered a REIT it must meet some conditions:

- Distribute, in the form of a dividend, at least 90% of the profits subject to taxation among its shareholders.

- Invest at least 75% of your assets in real estate, mortgage loans, stocks of other REITs (but < 25%) and cash.

- Receive at least 75% of your gross income from rentals, mortgage interest collection, or real estate sales.

- Have a minimum of 100 shareholders and no more than 50% of the shares are held by 5 or fewer shareholders.

- Be directed by a board of directors or trust that supervises the executive management of the company. Be a taxable entity

What types of REITs are there?

Fundamentally we can find two main types of REIT depending on your investment:

- Equity REITs invest directly in the purchase of properties and seek to generate returns through rentals and sales of real estate. This type of REIT is the most common (over 90%) and on which we will focus our study.

- Mortgage REITs invests in mortgages and financial products derived from them (they seek returns by financing their construction and through the interest on loans).

They were the most common type of REITs in the 1960s and 1970s, but the sharp rise in interest rates in '73 made many homeowners unable to afford their mortgages and defaults wiped out most of this type.

The biggest difficulty in valuing the products they own (credits) compared to direct ownership of the real estate, together with a higher level of leverage (debt-to-equity ratio) makes them more volatile values. They are also much more sensitive to interest rates than REITs that invest directly in real estate ownership. Therefore, this type of REITs tends to be a more volatile investment, with higher dividend yields, but also with greater risk than those investing directly in properties.

In each of these groups, we can find listed REITs, public but unlisted REITs, and private REITs.

- Listed REITs are registered with the SEC (the regulator of the American market) and their shares are listed on one of the US markets (many of them on the NYSE). These are companies subject to the same financial reporting and transparency requirements as other listed companies (quarterly and audited annual accounts). They are the REITs in which we can invest buying your shares like any other company.

- Public but unlisted REITs are those that are registered with the SEC and therefore must meet most of the requirements for listed companies but are not listed on any U.S. stock market. They are not so liquid, they usually have a certain minimum amount in the purchase of shares and the commissions tend to be higher (they are OTC markets, "over the counter").

- Private REITs are mostly intended for institutional investors, they are unlisted, and it is normally not possible to buy small packages of shares, but there are high minimum purchase requirements.

Finally, we can hear about UPREITs and DownREITs, which refer to a couple of similar REITs organizations, in which REITs do not directly own the properties but interests (participations) in an MLP that actually owns the properties (MLP "Master Limited Partnership" is a very common type of U.S. company to invest in energy infrastructure companies such as oil or gas pipelines. Perhaps it has a direct translation in Spain, but it is like a kind of "community of owners").

- UPREITs refers to "Umbrella Partnership REIT" because the REIT acts as an umbrella covering the structure of companies below. It was started to be used so that companies that already owned real estate could adopt the structure of a REIT without having to sell these properties to a new company created as REIT, with the consequent payment of taxes for probable capital gains.

- DownREITs are similar structures in which fundamentally the difference is that the REIT management has no interest (shares) in the MLP (only the REIT) whereas in the previous one it is usual that it does.

These structures give a fiscal advantage in case of asset sales and it is that on many occasions exchanges of interests (participations) are made between different REITs of their MLPs in such a way that they diversify their portfolio without having to buy/sell and therefore pay taxes.

And what are SOCIMIs? How do they resemble REITs?

SOCIMIs is the Spanish equivalent of American REITs (REITs or equivalents exist in about 40 countries worldwide). It is a type of society with similar characteristics that was created a few years ago in Spain to try to fill this gap, looking for a way to encourage investment in a sector that was being devastated by the crisis (they were created in 2009, although the law was reformed in 2013 and it has been after this modification when it has had a certain boom).

The main difference that exists with the REITs USA is the youth of the SOCIMIs, as opposed to companies with a history of more than 30 years of growing results and distribution of dividends, we have companies that are still creating portfolios, that still barely generate income, that has not distributed dividends (some have announced that they are going to do so soon), and so on. In other words, we are facing a much greater risk if we consider the investment in these companies than in their American "colleagues".

On the other hand, we may also be faced with a unique opportunity to invest in a business with a great future that is forming now and therefore may quote at prices that are laughing compared to what they have in a few years.

These are companies that should not have in their balance sheets junk (assets of little value at a gold price) corresponding to the real estate bubble period of a few years ago. They are new companies that have formed their real estate portfolios in a period of acute crisis in the real estate sector. In other words, if they have done it well, they have begun to buy properties at prices well below their real value and this in a few years should give some interesting returns.

Everyone must weigh their investments a lot, perhaps it is not a bad idea to look for a position in the Spanish SOCIMI, but always a very small part of the portfolio and trying to look for the ones with the highest quality assets.

Chapter 3: MAKE MONEY WITHOUT MONEY?

It's possible to make money without having money. The people who read this article are here because they want to know how to make money without having an initial capital to invest.

The answer is that you can start investing in real estate to generate profits without having a capital because the first thing you should invest in this business is time, knowledge and work. Mario Esquivel, author of the best-seller "Earn money without money in real estate" is one of the people who best knows and applies the new real estate paradigm. He explains that anyone without the need to invest money can generate wealth in this market and where the barriers of entry to this sector, due to lack of technical knowledge and previous experience, were believed to be unattainable for the normal citizen.

Mario Esquivel shares that initial capital is not the most important thing to enter this sector and generate profits. At this moment you must calculate the exact time in which you will have your performance and profit (from three to six months) controlling exactly what you will earn in each business or operation that you manage to do.

The real estate business involves thousands of people who seek to earn money in this way, through the negotiation of real estate. This is a model to earn money without money in real estate, most people who are located in this sector, are immersed in a "red ocean" where the competition is huge, brutal and profit margins are narrower with the passage of time, but what we have to look for, are the "blue oceans" which are the niches that are not very exploited and you can start looking for information, having the belief that you can become an investor and this has to be your main objective. There are blue oceans now, there have been and will continue to be in the future, it is only a matter of knowing how to find them, know the supply, demand and act, always seeking to manage market information which is a very important point to take into account.

How can we start trading in this market without having money to invest and generate profits?

Easy, we will focus especially and strongly on the part of selling (All those people who need to sell their property by placing it in the market) and on the multiple offers that exist in the market. For this, we will have to select the properties that fulfill certain requirements which will help us to carry out a faster operation.

To start looking for an operation, we must rely on digital systems. In each country, it is easy to find websites in which many real estate markets are published, which allow us to optimize our time and it is not necessary to publish on these sites, here we can select a property that has potential and can take some time already in the market without any success.

It is proposed to the seller of the property that has been in the market for some time, to offer to solve the problem of lack of demand, that is, the lack of potential customers who can visit the property and show interest. We all know that a restored property is easier and quicker to sell. If the seller does not have the money for the reform, you can be the one who offers him the idea of investing in his property, you will oversee carrying out the reforms and making a contract of association in the participation of the property. The benefit that you can obtain in each operation that you achieve you have to base it on having a margin that is sufficient to support it to the cost of the reform, is fair and gives to the operation a win-win to all the parts that are included: seller, buyer and you as an associated investor.

There are a lot of ideas and concepts that you can use in a home to improve its purchasing potential, the most advisable is to put everything in the refurbishment of the kitchen and bathrooms, which are important points for potential buyers.

The association agreement determines the economic conditions that will be applied once the sale has taken place, in other words, the benefit that will interest you.

So far so good but who will suffer the reforms of the property if you do not have the money in the first operations? For this, you must find a reform company that trusts you and that you trust and can reach a deferred payment agreement (an estimated time of 3 months is a reasonable measure) and that you can leverage the money. If you exceed the agreed time limit and the property has not been sold, the reform company will apply surcharges that will reduce your profit at the time of the sale of the property.

Is this form of leverage possible?

Of course, it is possible, the secret is to determine and make agreements win-win, to all parties involved in the business. This is where your facet of negotiator and salesman must come in.

One risk that needs to be addressed in this type of business is ensuring that the seller of the property pays what was agreed in the contract when the property is sold. It is for this that the acceptance on the part of the salesperson must be concretized to make a signature of legal document that commits him in the operation, this is a document of the type "promissory note with guarantee". This way we will be giving a solution to a real problem that has the seller of a property that needs money is tired of waiting and this way we assure that it is a win-win formula for both parts. You as an investor must have the guarantee of your investment (leveraging third party money) and the seller must know that if he does not pay, you will execute the accepted guarantee, i.e. the promissory note or the guarantee. If the seller does not accept this contract formula do not worry, it is very

24

sure that you will find many other owners who are willing to formulate a win-win agreement with you, just keep looking.

Is it simple? Yeah, is it easy? OH, NO.

It's not easy because, to articulate a model like the one described above, you have to leave your comfort zone and put yourself to the test looking for what you want to win-win. You should not give up; this is an extremely difficult investment model but if you can catch the pace you will get big profits.

Is this a valid business model for anyone?

No, this is not a business model that anyone can run, but it does not mean that there is only one type of person who can run this type of business. To carry out this type of business you must know how to surround yourself with people who know how to manage the legal, tax and also real estate appraisers.

Here's a story about a person who invested in real estate with no money to accomplish his goal. The story begins like this:

"Don't say I can't, instead say, what can I do?"

Santiago begins the story of how he bought his motorcycle working in real estate and has a message to say, which is: YES IT CAN! We must not be negative by saying it can't be done. We must change our way of thinking, asking ourselves how and what should I do. God gave all humans gifts, talents and there they are. It's up to us to see how we train ourselves to know how to use them in our lives.

My anecdote of the purchase of the motorcycle, was of those things that have a purpose, "I believe that there is nothing by chance, in everything, God has a purpose".

It happened because a group of friends, members of the Christian congregation I attend, invited me to go out with them for a motorcycle ride. They lent me a small 125 CC "messenger" motorcycle, which took me to the Panamanian border 325 kilometers away.

I accompanied them, but of course, they traveled with powerful machines of more than 800 CC, big, comfortable, fast, and elegant. They say I was going for a hundred, but "praying." That situation prompted me to purchase my motorcycle, which cost approximately $6000, in 2013.

At first I said, "I can't buy the motorcycle, I don't have any money". However, I remembered that in "Rich

Dad, Poor Dad", Kiyosaki, mentioned that one should not say NO, but rather ask oneself:

What do I want the motorcycle for?

What do I have to do to get the money?

The "reality" was that in my context, there were few (and expensive) possibilities to get the money needed to buy the bike. After doing a mini brainstorm to analyze how to get the money, my options were:

I was able to get a loan, but at quite high-interest rates, which ranged between 18 and 22%, a situation that I dismissed with very little analysis. I discarded it, on the one hand, because of the high interest and on the other because I was acquiring a liability, which did not put money in my pocket.

Find a new job.

They were all discarded, as he was not willing to borrow, and did not want to work anymore, as he was retired. The alternatives were getting smaller and smaller.

For eight days, I asked myself: *Do you want the bike, would you like to buy it? What good will it do you?*

The responses were positive:

Yes, I want it, yes, it will serve me as a means of transportation, hobby, and will save me fuel. (With my car, I spent $100 per month, and with the bike, I would spend $12, huge difference). It all came down to one question:

How to honestly get the money, without acquiring bad debts?

One fine morning, in radiant sunshine, as I walked, I read on a sign: "Owner selling lot, no middleman".

I took the telephone number on the sign and inquired with the owner who he was, where he lived, how many meters the lot was, what the value of the lot was, conditions of sale, and so on.

Once I had the data, I looked for a meeting with him to get to know us, and I took the opportunity to tell him that I could find him a buyer, but of course, as long as there was a commission, which we agreed on a 5% on the sale, which would give me about $4,000.

And as they say... The one who has the information has the power.

I soon became aware of a possible buyer, with whom I met and told him that I could get him a lot and, given my relationship with the banks through some of my students, I could also give him access to part of the credit if he needed it. The deal was that if the business was done, he was to give me a $2,000 commission. He accepted the agreement.

I set up this negotiation within 30 days and waited another 30 days for the bank to make the disbursement to the buyer.

Both gentlemen fulfilled their promises, without signed documents, and that is how today I have my 800 CC Suzuki motorcycle, which I enjoy every day, traveling even to other countries like Nicaragua, Panama, but especially in my beautiful Costa Rica, full of sun, sand and sea.

This is one of those businesses where there is only the possibility of win-win, where we win the 3 participants (owner, buyer and this server intermediary). I believe that real estate is an easy, clean and fast way to earn money, you don't need money to do business, just the information of who sells and who buys.

Also, I believe that it is universal, it takes place anywhere in the world, with similar circumstances in all countries. For many people it can be the business of a lifetime, if they work fairly, transparently and honestly, the rest will prosper God.

I invite you to use the gifts that God gave you abundantly and freely, and for which one day He will ask us: What did you do with the gifts that I gave you? I hope that in your case, God will say to you: "Well done, good and faithful servant".

Thanks for reading my story.

-Santiago Rodriguez

Tips and another example of investment without money:

Define what you want

When I bought my first apartment, I was sure I didn't necessarily want to live in it. I wanted to invest my savings in something that would generate income for me later without much effort. Since I'm not good with Forex, I didn't even think in chain sales that real estate would be the best thing for me: you buy a house you just rent it out.

You have to think about maintenance costs, emergencies (leaks, broken pipes, bad tenants) and taxes, but if you compare the time invested with the income, the profit is a lot. If you're investing in real estate for the first time, think about whether you want that place to be your home or whether you want to rent for income.

When you buy a house, you are thinking about your perfect home, the neighborhood you like the most, a spacious, functional, etc. Now, that perfect place may be out of your budget, but it doesn't matter why. Decide what you want to invest for and start by placing your dream within the real.

Start small:

When I set about buying my first apartment, I researched what I needed. I visited several banks to find out my creditworthiness, how much they could lend me, and how much I should have for my down payment.

Since I already had some money saved, I took out the calculator and realized that I couldn't buy something, for example, for $100 million, which left out of my range several possibilities. The bank only lent me for something of $70 million and I had to have 30% of that value as a down payment.

I did not have any housing subsidy (as exists in several parts) that could provide me with extra income. With my savings and a little help, I managed to complete the down payment, so I went to the bank for a pre-approval.

With the green light from the bank, the hunt began (which lasted about seven months). It was clear to me that I was going to buy something within my budget to have a small fee that would not take all of my paychecks and leave me the ability to save to pay as quickly as possible. And I got it!

I bought a small apartment, under my budget, in a good place and very cozy. It wasn't exactly the place where I aspired to live but it was something very good within what I could afford.

What I mean by this is that, when it comes to investing, you don't necessarily have to buy the mansion of your dreams. It also doesn't mean that your first purchase is going to be your home for life.

Look at it only as a small investment that in the future will give you the chance to buy something bigger and better. Look for something economic, that fits your income and that after a few months is not a torture to pay. If the fee steals half your salary and that means you'll have to fill your credit card quota, make terrible sacrifices or borrow more to survive, it's not worth it.

Carefully review how much you can give in monthly payments and whether it gives you room to save and make capital payments. Visit several banks and get advice from people who already own homes to make the right decision.

Let the debts pay themselves!

This is my favorite part! You can make the debts pay themselves, which sounds illogical, but it is. When you buy a house, don't live in it, rent it out and the rent will pay for itself.

So, I did, at first, I had to put some more money, but as I was making payments the fee was decreasing. During that time, of course, I had to make several sacrifices: I lived in rented rooms or with my parents, which is cheaper than renting a house and freed me from utility costs.

On the other hand, I got an extra job which made me work ten hours a day from Monday to Saturday. It was exhausting but it was only for two years. In this time, I saved everything that my extra work produced and with it I was able to make installments to the capital decreasing more and more the payments and, best of all, I was already beginning to surplus money!

This was the decision I made. I lived a little tight during that time, but I always had something for a quiet vacation. All of this was the product of my planning. Other alternatives, once you acquire a property, can be:

- Renting one or more rooms: having housemates can be fun or a nightmare, it's up to you to choose the inhabitants of your house. Look how you advance in this option and sacrifice a little, it does not mean that it will be like this for the rest of your life. That extra income will make your life easier in the future.

- Renovate a part of your parents' house, so you can live there. The cost of the loan will be lower, and you will be in a place that will be yours once you decide the terms of the property with your parents. The good thing about most families is that they are always willing to contribute to the well-being of their children, so it may be a plus for you.

- Buy a house that already has an apartment or separate space. Some buildings, especially large houses, have a studio apartment, or a first floor that works independently of the main building. Rent it out and you'll have a house with two benefits in one!

- Rent out the garage. In the city I lived in, it was common for garages to adapt as separate studios. All you had to do was put in a small kitchen, a bathroom and that's it! You have a separate room with a good income to rent.

- Use Airbnb: join this program and rent your house to tourists.

Chapter 4: Tips for Investing in Real Estate

Location

The value of a property depends largely on its location. Having a studio apartment in an exclusive sector is better than having a giant house in the worst neighborhood in the city. Analyze where you want to buy access roads, public transport, proximity to shopping centers or recreation areas. Some factors, such as being in front of a busy road, can diminish the value of a property.

Evaluate the market

Research different real estate prices of rents, utilities, and taxes to get an idea of your profit margin. This way you will be able to have the clearest accounts about how much you should put or exceed when renting. Ask about the sectors that are growing or where public works are being built that will allow you to increase the price of your property in the future. You could sell later and make a lot more money.

State of the property

Check carefully the property you want to buy, the state of the structure, bathrooms, doors, kitchen, etc. If there is something that needs renovation you can negotiate a discount. It is also important to ask who the neighbors are for because no one wants noisy or troubled people around them.

Buy to remodel

If you like interior design, this is a good option, plus the property comes out cheaper. If this option catches your attention, make a renewal budget with an expert (remember to put 10% as budgets are never accurate) and see how good business it is. This can be another business option: buy cheap, remodel and sell more expensive.

Bank auctions

Banks constantly seize property for non-payment. Those same properties then sell them cheaper on the market, so they become a real bargain. Before you buy, check the local banks for their auctions.

Buy a piece of land and build

Sometimes building can be cheaper than buying done. Research and budget this option.

Don't buy off-plan

When you buy off-plan you have the advantage of having more time to pay the down payment, but that means two or three years of dead money. If you buy something ready to rent, you can start making money from day one. You are also subject to delays in the delivery of the work, extra costs as they do not deliver the terminations or perhaps theft.

Think long term

Remember that a property won't make you rich overnight. It's a process that takes time (but time flies!) but little by little it will help you build a stable income and a small fortune.

We will analyze the case of Robert Kiyosaki

Kiyosaki became interested in a $100,000 property. When he began managing to acquire it and negotiated an excellent cash price of $80,000 (this shows why he became one of the best sellers at Xerox, for his bargaining power to both buy and sell). Of the $80,000 he only had $10,000 and to make up the shortfall, he applied for a bank loan of $70,000.

To be able to sell the furniture in a short time, he published a very tempting ad (this ad would make me want to call him right now):

"House for sale. Desperate owner. No bank authorization is required. Low down payment, easy monthly payments.

Wow! This ad is great, just need to say, "come with a die and if you get a 3 you get it for free!".

Fact: By the time Kiyosaki was performing these operations, he says it took between 1 and 4 weeks to complete them, from the time he bought until he sold.

The case numbers:

- 100.000 It's the market value of the house.

- 80,000 is the price at which you buy it.

- 10,000 is what Kiyosaki puts into his savings for the purchase of the house.

- 70,000 is the loan Kiyosaki takes from the bank.

He got a buyer for the house in less than a month who was willing to pay 100,000 but in installments, so it would be 100,000 plus interest.

To secure the business, Kiyosaki implemented a contract with a guarantee for 100,000 (which does not mean that it was sold for 100,000, it is only a sum to have as a guarantee). If the buyer stopped paying at some point, Kiyosaki could sell the property back to another, without having to return the money paid so far.

Kiyosaki explains:

"The net effect is that I have created $30,000 in my asset column for which I will be paid interest.

The explanation of how he is going to charge interest on the 30,000 he mentions does not end well, but we can analyze it. Let's go back to the numbers to refresh them:

- 80.000 It's the price for which you buy the property.

- 10,000 is what Kiyosaki puts into his savings for the purchase of the house.

- 70,000 is the loan Kiyosaki takes from the bank.

- 100,000 + interest is the value at which the real estate sells, but almost everything in installments (although the guarantee is for 100,000).

To make the example simple and clear:

- Suppose the bank charges you 10% interest (annual) on the 70,000 loans.

- Suppose Kiyosaki charges the house buyer an advance of 10,000.

- Suppose Kiyosaki charges the house buyer the same interest rate as the banks charge, 10% (annual) for the remaining 90,000.

- Let us suppose that Kiyosaki finances the full payment of the one-year installments.

Note: the choice of a 10% annual interest, is to make the numbers round.

The situation is seen from the bank employee's side:

He sees this type of operation happening every day, but he doesn't enter any of them, he simply receives a salary at the end of the month. If you don't show up every day for work, you don't get paid.

The situation as seen from the bank's side:

-   Earn 10% a year out of 70,000, which equals 7,000.

(This should be paid by Kiyosaki, although later I show how he did to pay interest only for 60,000).

The situation is seen from the buyer's side of the real estate:

-   You have to pay only 10,000 in advance

-   Get 90,000 in the financing, paying Kiyosaki interest at 10% per annum (9,000)

-   Since Kiyosaki provides the financing, it does not require as much paperwork as a bank would ask.

The purchase can be almost immediate and the interest Kiyosaki charges you, is the same as a bank.

The situation as seen from Kiyosaki's side:

-   The 10,000 you put into your savings to pay for the property is requested from the new buyer as an advance. So, he recovered that 10,000 in less than a month.

- With that 10,000 you can advance fees to the bank. The loan I had taken out was 70,000 - 10,000 (advancing). Now he only owes 60,000.

- The remaining 60,000 of the credit you requested from the bank + your interest, is being paid with the installments paid by the new buyer of the house. It would be like "transferring" credit to the new buyer. I put "transfer" between quotation marks because this transfer is not made in the papers.

- Earn 20,000 for buying at 80,000 and selling at 100,000.

- He earns interest on the 20,000 he earned on the buy-sell + 10,000 he put in. Interest is 10% per annum, so 10% of 30,000 = 3000.

Difference between Capital Gain and Assets

The 20,000 you earned by making a sale is a CAPITAL PROFIT.

The 3,000 you earned from interest are earnings generated by an ASSET. Every month he put money in his pocket without doing anything else.

Summary

Basically, what he did was first win 20,000 for the rebate he could get. Then leverage money from the bank and somehow transfer the credit payment to the new buyer. Then he charged interest on those 20,000 he earned and charged interest on 10,000 he put out of his pocket.

Once you got your 10,000 back, why did you advance fees to the bank? He did it so he could collect, interest on that 10,000 instead of the bank. If he did not advance them, the bank would charge interest for 70,000, but as he advanced them, the bank would only charge interest for 60,000, the interest for the remaining 10,000 he kept.

If I had to do a similar business but without leveraging the bank, I only had 10,000 in hand, so I could only earn 10% of that sum = 1,000 in a year. And from winning 1,000 he went on to win 23,000 for using the bank as leverage. What a difference!

Intermediating in real estate operations

An intermediary in the real estate market is the profession usually practiced by agents in the sector who, by meditating in each sale or rent property, charge a commission. The role of intermediary or advisor in real estate investments well done will be a way of making profits. "The key to success is the product," says Flores, "a good intermediary is one who makes a good catchment task and has a good product, such as exclusive pieces in prime locations, renting small, reduced-price housing in large cities, apartments or bank flats that are at a good price and can be financed 100%. To do this, you must know the market and the customer.

Although agent Antonio J. Berzal Otero reminds us that "only through intermediaries do we invest less than by buying and selling, but we always invest". To begin in the profession, the real estate franchises open the doors to the self-employed. "I'm a freelance REMAX agent because it's like you have a real estate agency of your own with minimal structural costs. Frankly a good system," advises Berzal. Forming, making contacts and moving within a circle of investors is the way to start and gain experience.

Transforming a warehouse or premises into a dwelling

The cost of commercial premises has historically always been lower than that of housing. Therefore, by making a reliable calculation of the money it costs to buy one of these warehouses and the integral works of transformation in housing and its adaptation to the requirements of the Technical Building Code (CTE), it will be analyzed if it is good business. It is advisable to previously study the demand for a local market to make sure that it will have demand.

Later, a decorator or architect could be hired to calculate the cost of this transformation and provide us with digital infographics that would help us enormously with our investor client. Finally, to advise you on setting the selling price, a good method is to advertise through the most frequented sales channels (Internet, street signs, real estate portals, etc.) to find the price that potential investors would pay for each of the lofts. All this useful information could be sold in a dossier to an investor and charged a fee.

Buy real estate debt and negotiate with the bank

Bank debt and evictions keep going up. Many developers, investors or ordinary people with more than five properties are therefore in danger of being repossessed by the bank. In these cases, the investor can buy all the bank debt from the owner and then negotiate with the bank.

"If we are presented with any developer or investor with a lot of bank-debt property, we could pay a big commission to buy it from them or help them make it profitable through renting," explains Haro.

Vulture fund strategy? These situations may not be the best fit for the seller, but it may be a less bad way out before you fall into foreclosure or a lifelong debt that causes you to fall into bankruptcy.

Manage third party wealth or financing

Being a good negotiator and knowledgeable of the sector, you will be prepared to make profitable the own capital of third parties. "You can invest small amounts of large capital in various niches in the sector, such as the stock exchange, i.e. 3,000 euros, 4,000 euros or more in real estate business and become someone who earns money by investing. The SOCIMI, which devote their activity mainly to obtaining profitability in the rental market, are increasingly presented as the best option, with accessibility through the Alternative Stock Market (MAB). But first it is advisable to be informed and advised: "It is a good option for the liquidity they offer, for diversification and the possibility of access with initially small amounts," says Flores in this regard.

In terms of managing the best use of an owner's property, we are talking about a role very similar to that of the property manager, that is, taking care of the financial, legal and technical matters necessary for its maintenance. Taking charge of renting it, demanding the collection of the rents or taking charge of conserving the flat (reforms, supplies, security...), while it remains empty or for sale.

It is necessary to have professional management of them.

Now that you have read about real estate investment systems, their different models, examples of people who have managed to get riches by taking advantage of information and you have a basic idea of how to get into the real estate business, you have to know how to start working from this legally, that is why I bring you a little guide so that you know how to become a real estate agent.

Being at this point we can ask ourselves then what is the best way we can start in the real estate business?

There are countless answers to this question, but we must always bear in mind that to start in this business we must act as an intermediary and put all our knowledge into it.

Why Real Estate Intermediation?

- You can start doing it in your free time.

- There is a financial risk of zero (0).

- There are practically no start-up costs.

- You don't need to have a capital to get started.

- You can determine if investing in real estate is your thing, before investing hundreds of thousands of dollars in books or courses.

Your job will be to provide information on qualified prospects and the investor's job is to manage the rest of the process.

- You'll win while you learn the business.

For each business referred by you that the investor closes, you will be receiving a commission already squared between you and the others involved in the business.

There are several ways to make agreements in which you can benefit greatly:

- Set a fixed rate of gain.

- Establish a percentage of profit from the acquired property.

- A net gain.

- Commissions combining more than one of the above methods.

Build relationships with mentors.

No doubt having a mentor is the most efficient way to learn, but it can be difficult to find a mentor who wants to work with you, so you should try to learn as much as you can from the people who work in this field.

In general, experienced investors do not have time to mentor all those who request it, so you should make the most of the time you can have to talk to an experienced person, remember that information is the key to success.

Build your team

It's smarter to have professionals on your side to give you proper advice. Make sure your team of lawyers, builders, accountants, engineers and all the other experts who will have to work with you are well trained and qualified.

Start the activity in your free time

You can take advantage of that free time you have to start working as a real estate intermediary, by providing excellent quality prospects you are saving your investor time and helping them earn money.

You can work in this business from the comfort of your home and without having to give up your current job, what you must keep in mind is to do much of the online market research to get information.

As you gain experience, you will work closer and closer to your investors and you will learn firsthand how the business works.

As time passes you should be able to take the next step where you will know how to find profitable businesses. As an experienced investor, you'll have the ability to find motivated salespeople, that's one aspect that doesn't change in this business.

Know how to Network

It is also important for you to meet and communicate regularly with other property investors who may be able to give you some useful tips and you will be informed of current trends in the real estate industry. You can achieve this by using social networks which will facilitate the search for information and the ability to create contacts for future business.

How to be a successful intermediary?

You must recognize the needs of your investors, know what type of properties you manage, the price range and what locations you are looking for and prefer. The investor is your client and it is your duty to give him or her what they want, to get what we are looking for that is win-win. You must conduct an extensive and thorough investigation before investing in any area or property. You'll want to know the costs of renting a property in a given area, the income and lifestyle of people in that area, their taste and buying preferences, zoning laws and other necessary information that would guide your investment.

CONCLUSION

When reading this book you will realize the great number of ways that can be used to generate income through this business, you will understand that it is not necessary to have the start up capital to enter the real estate world and that the fundamental thing is to have the greatest amount of information about the active market.

In the long run, the most important asset most people have when they retire is the capital that represents their own home. According to an article that appeared several years ago in Reader's Digest, the average net worth of a typical American homeowner was $63,000. The average net worth of the typical tenant was only $1,921. About 30 times less. You must get a home of your own. And if you've already bought it, you have to learn how to turn it into a money-making machine.

Even if property values don't continue to rise, you'll learn the proper techniques for buying properties so below their value that you won't mind if some of the prices in your city go up again.

For now, all you need to understand is that there is no such investment as real estate in versatility and power.

The best time to buy real estate is TODAY and that's not going to change in the short term. Your home will continue to be not only your castle, but also your bank, your cash machine, your mandatory savings bank, and your vehicle for a quick retirement and the lifestyle of your dreams.